Early
ANIMAL
Encyclopedias

HORSES

by Marne Ventura

Early Encyclopedias

An Imprint of Abdo Reference
abdobooks.com

abdobooks.com

Published by Abdo Reference, a division of ABDO, PO Box 398166, Minneapolis, Minnesota 55439.
Copyright © 2023 by Abdo Consulting Group, Inc. International copyrights reserved in all countries.
No part of this book may be reproduced in any form without written permission from the
publisher. Early Encyclopedias™ is a trademark and logo of Abdo Reference.

Printed in the United States of America, North Mankato, Minnesota.
102022
012023

Editor: Marie Pearson
Series Designers: Candice Keimig, Joshua Olson

Library of Congress Control Number: 2022940649

Publisher's Cataloging-in-Publication Data

Names: Ventura, Marne, author.
Title: Horses / by Marne Ventura
Description: Minneapolis, Minnesota: Abdo Publishing, 2023 | Series: Early animal encyclopedias |
      Includes online resources and index.
Identifiers: ISBN 9781098290436 (lib. bdg.) | ISBN 9781098275754 (ebook)
Subjects: LCSH: Horses--Juvenile literature. | Horses--Behavior--Juvenile literature. | Zoology--
      Juvenile literature. | Encyclopedias and dictionaries--Juvenile literature.
Classification: DDC 636.1--dc23

CONTENTS

Show ponies compete in horse shows.

What Are Horses?

Horses are mammals. They have hooves. They eat grasses, hay, and grains. Horses are measured in hands. One hand is 4 inches (10 cm). Horse hands are measured from the ground to the horse's withers. There are hundreds of breeds of horses. Different breeds are good at doing different things.

Ponies are the smallest horses. They are under 14.2 hands. Ponies are strong, sturdy, and smart. They can

Some light horses help move cattle.

carry or pull heavy loads. Ponies can be stubborn and spirited. Children and small adults sometimes ride ponies.

Light horses are medium-sized. They are used for riding, racing, jumping, and moving livestock. They run fast on their long legs. Their backs are the right shape to hold a saddle.

Draft horses are big and heavy. They pull plows and wagons. They carry heavy loads. Their legs are short and sturdy. They have strong muscles in their backs and legs.

Draft horses can pull plows.

Horse Colors and Patterns

Horses come in a variety of colors. Some horses are palominos. They have cream to golden coats. Their manes and tails are lighter than their bodies. Chestnuts have red bodies, manes, and tails. Bay horses have brown bodies. Their manes, tails, muzzles, and legs are black. Black horses are all black. Gray horses are born a dark color. As they age, they turn light gray or white.

Buckskin horses have golden coats. Their manes, tails, and lower legs are black. A dun horse is tan or gray. It has a black stripe along its back. The mane, tail, and lower legs are black.

Horses come in several patterns too. Roan horses have white hairs mixed in with colored hairs. Pinto horses have colored coats with patches of white. Some horses have spots. Horses can also have white markings on their heads and legs.

Horse Colors

Chestnut

Bay

Gray

Black

Dun

Palomino

Horse Patterns

Buckskin

Roan

Pinto

AKHAL-TEKE

Akhal-Tekes form strong relationships with their owners.

Appearance

The Akhal-Teke stands straight and tall. Its head, neck, back, and legs are long. Its mane is silky and short. Its tail is also short. Akhal-Tekes can be dun, bay, gray, or golden. Their manes and tails are dark.

Height: 15 to 15.1 hands

Behavior and Uses

Akhal-Tekes come from Turkmenistan, a country in Central Asia. Akhal-Tekes have been used by soldiers and for racing for 3,000 years. They are known for bravery in war. They can keep up their energy for a long time. Today, Akhal-Tekes are used in horse shows. They are known for their beauty and intelligence. They are good jumpers.

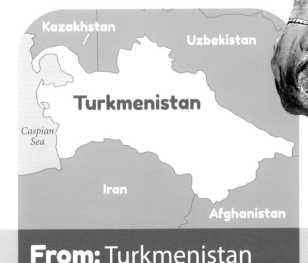

From: Turkmenistan

AMERICAN BASHKIR CURLY

The Bashkir curly's short summer coat can look almost straight.

Appearance

The American Bashkir curly has a thick coat of curly hair. It is medium-sized. It can be any common horse color. This horse has wide-set eyes. Its hooves are black. It has a short back.

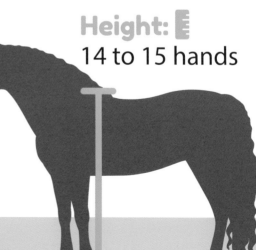

Height:
14 to 15 hands

Behavior and Uses

The American Bashkir curly was first found in the mountains of Nevada. The horse sheds its fur in summer. Its coat becomes wavy or straight. The mane and tail grow back in the winter. So do the curls on the body. Winter coat patterns can look like velvet. Sometimes the coat curls are ringlets. Curlies are calm and gentle. They can be good riding horses for beginners.

From: The United States of America

AMERICAN PAINT HORSE

If white does not cross a paint horse's back, the pattern is called overo.

Appearance

The American paint horse has patches of two colors. One is white. The second color can be different shades of black, bay, brown, gray, or roan. Paints are stocky and muscular. Each horse has its own

Height: 14 to 16 hands

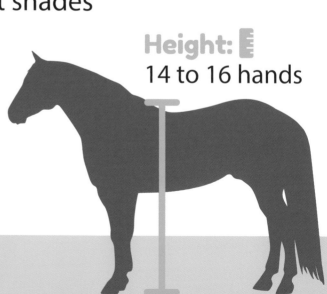

special color pattern. Some have more white than color. Others have more color than white.

Behavior and Uses

Spanish explorers brought horses with patches of color to the Americas hundreds of years ago. People decided to make horses with this pattern a breed in the mid-1900s. Paints came from American quarter horses and Thoroughbreds. They are smart and easy to train. Today, they are used for riding, showing, ranching, and rodeos. They are gentle with children.

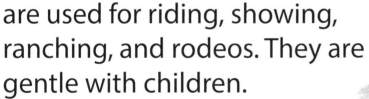

From: The United States of America

AMERICAN QUARTER HORSE

Quarter horses are powerful.

Appearance

The American quarter horse is often seen in Western movies and TV shows. It can be reddish brown, bay, black, chestnut, or gray. It has heavy muscles.

Behavior and Uses

The American quarter horse is from the

Height:
14.3 to 15.1 hands

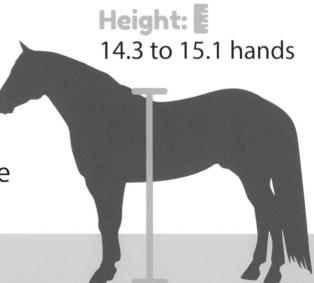

United States. It has a gentle nature. Quarter horses have been used by cowboys and ranchers for many years. They are good at moving cattle from one place to another. They can round up cattle too. People also use them in horse shows, for racing, or to ride for fun. The quarter horse got its name because it can run one-quarter of a mile (0.4 km) very quickly.

From: The United States of America

AMERICAN SADDLEBRED

American saddlebreds often look proud.

Appearance

The American saddlebred is known for its beauty. It has a short, strong back. Its neck is long and thin. It can be different colors with white markings.

Behavior and Uses

People have ridden American saddlebreds

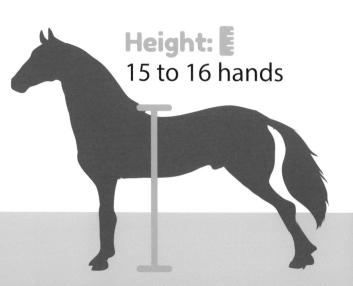

Height: 15 to 16 hands

since the 1800s. These horses were used by soldiers, farmers, and settlers. Today, American saddlebreds are often used as show horses. They are known for their gaits. A gait is a special way of walking. American saddlebreds can walk, trot, and canter. They also have a gait where they raise each foot high between steps. American saddlebreds are used to pull carts. They are used for show jumping. People also ride them for fun.

From: The United States of America

ANDALUSIAN

The Andalusian has a short back.

Appearance

The Andalusian is usually white or light gray. Sometimes it is bay. The horse's mane and tail are thick. It has big eyes. Its muzzle is flat, and its ears are small. The neck is long and thick. The Andalusian's chest is big, and its hips are lean.

France

Portugal

Spain

Atlantic Ocean

Mediterranean Sea

Morocco

From: Portugal and Spain

Behavior and Uses

People have been riding Andalusians since the Middle Ages (500–1500 CE). Soldiers rode them in battle. After the Middle Ages, they were used in horse shows. Later, Europeans brought them to what is now the United States. Andalusians are quick learners. They are smart and easygoing. People use them today for ranching, competitions, and parades.

Height:
15.2 to 16.2 hands

Every Appaloosa's pattern is unique.

Appearance

The Appaloosa can have many different coat patterns. It can be chestnut, bay, gray, or black. It is often covered with splashes and spots of white. Sometimes it has a white base covered with splashes of darker color. The horse's skin is also spotted with

Height: 14 to 16 hands

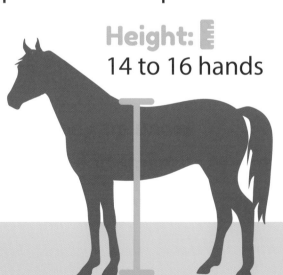

dark and light colors. Many Appaloosas have striped hooves.

Behavior and Uses

American Indians bred Appaloosas when white settlers first brought horses to North America. The horses were fast and steady runners. Appaloosas are often ridden in events like roping or barrel racing. They make good ranch or trail horses. Some pull carts, and people ride others for fun.

From: North America

The Arabian is known for its beauty.

Appearance

The Arabian has a long, arched neck. Its eyes and nostrils are big. Its muzzle is small. The Arabian has long shoulders and a broad chest. Its back is short. Arabians can be gray, chestnut, bay, or roan. Sometimes they are black.

Height:
14.2 to 15.2 hands

Behavior and Uses

Arabians were first bred in the deserts of the Middle East. People used them in battle. They were strong, brave, and fast. They came to North America in the 1700s. Arabians are now used to compete and perform in shows. They are good at races and long-distance rides. They are usually smart and friendly to people.

From: The Middle East

The Ardennes has short, powerful legs.

Appearance

The Ardennes can be bay, roan, chestnut, gray, or palomino. It has long hair around its lower legs and hooves. The horse is stocky and muscular. It has a short back, small ears, and a broad head.

Height: 14.2 to 16 hands

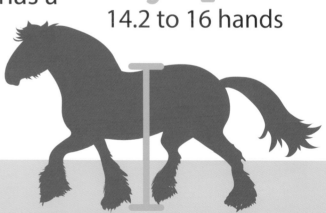

Behavior and Uses

The Ardennes has been used as a draft horse since the Middle Ages. It is named for a region in France. Ardennes are calm and easygoing. They are strong and tough. Farmers use them to pull plows or carts. These horses are hard workers. They do well in areas that are hilly or rough. They do not need special food, so they are easy to keep.

From: Europe

AUSTRALIAN BRUMBY

Wild Australian brumbies can be caught and trained.

Appearance

Brumby is the name given to a feral horse in Australia. The first Australian brumbies came from Australian draft horses and Thoroughbreds. Today, they are all different sizes and colors.

Coral Sea

Australia

Indian Ocean

Pacific Ocean

From: Australia

Behavior and Uses

Experts think that brumbies ran away or were left behind by ranchers in the late 1700s. The ranchers used them for farm work or for riding and pulling. Today, many ranchers see them as a problem. Some have become too wild to train. Some carry diseases. The horses damage fencing. They drain water sources and hurt ranch animals. People disagree about brumbies. Some think they are pests. Others think they should be protected.

Height: Varies

The Azteca's ancestors are Andalusians, Criollos, and quarter horses.

Appearance

The Azteca has a thin, medium-sized head. Its eyes and nostrils are big. Its mane is thick. This horse has a wide chest and a short back. The Azteca is strong and

Height: 14.1 to 15.3 hands

muscular. Its coat is shiny. An Azteca can be any color, without spots or patches.

Behavior and Uses

The Azteca is the first horse breed to come from Mexico. Aztecas are easy to train. They are often used for shows or to ride for fun. An Azteca is strong. It can work for a long time. These horses are good jumpers. Ranchers in Mexico ride them while roping cattle.

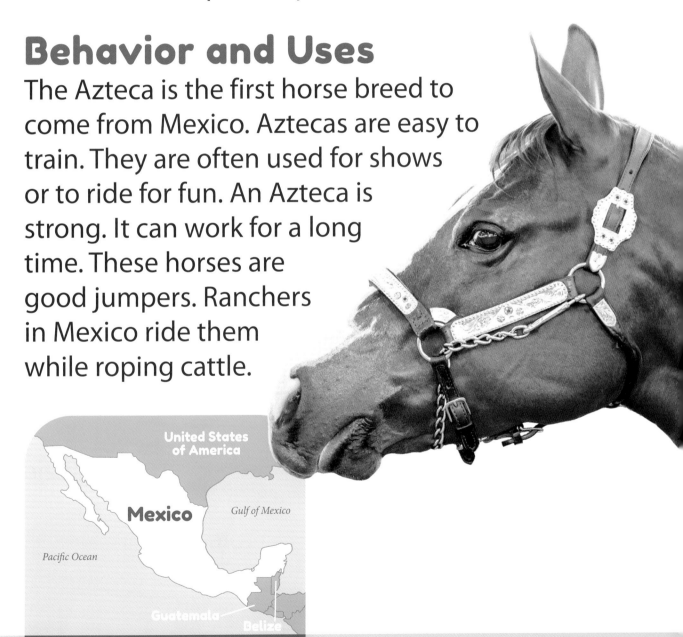

From: Mexico

BELGIAN

Belgians are good at farm work.

Appearance

The Belgian is a heavy draft horse. It can weigh more than 2,000 pounds (907 kg). This horse can be blonde, sorrel, roan, or chestnut. It usually has a light-colored mane and tail and a white stripe on its face. The Belgian is muscular and stocky.

Height: 16 to 18 hands

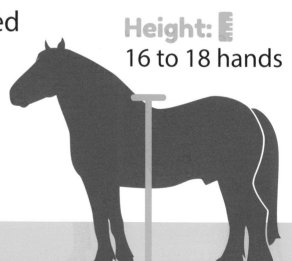

Behavior and Uses

Belgians come from the country of Belgium. They carried knights into battle during the Middle Ages. They became popular in the United States in the early 1900s. These horses worked on farms and ranches. They could pull heavy loads on carts and carriages. Today, they are often seen in shows and contests. Belgians are known for being gentle and tough.

The Canadian horse has a lively gait.

Appearance

The Canadian horse is most often black. It can also be dark brown, bay, or chestnut. The horse's broad face has straight lines. Its eyes are wide set. It has large nostrils. The Canadian horse has an arched neck. Its mane and tail are thick, long,

Height:
14 to 16 hands

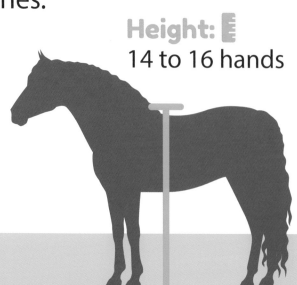

and wavy. The Canadian horse has strong legs. Its coat is soft and shiny.

Behavior and Uses

This horse is smart, friendly, and eager to please. Early settlers in the United States and Canada used this horse. They rode the horse and used it to pull farm equipment or carts. It was called the "little iron horse" because it was so strong and hardworking.

Canada

Pacific
Ocean

United States
of America

Atlantic
Ocean

From: Canada

The Caspian's nostrils are large.

Appearance

The Caspian has a short head and ears. Its eyes are large. Its muzzle is small. The neck is thin. This horse's back is straight, and it has a high tail. Its legs are slim.

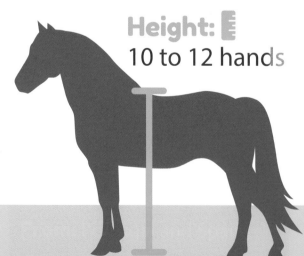

Height: 10 to 12 hands

A Caspian can be bay, chestnut, gray, or black. It is the size of some ponies. Experts call it a horse because its body is built more like a horse than a pony.

Behavior and Uses

People first used Caspians thousands of years ago in Iran. These horses pulled chariots. Today, the breed is very rare. Caspians are used in shows. They are good jumpers. They are also good at pulling carts. Caspians can be good horses for kids because of their small size.

From: Iran

CHINCOTEAGUE PONY

Experts think this breed is a horse whose poor diet keeps it from growing larger.

Appearance

The Chincoteague pony is a small, sturdy, shaggy horse. It has short legs, a thick mane, and a round belly. It comes in many colors and patterns.

Height: 12 to 13 hands

Behavior and Uses

These horses came to Assateague Island off the coast of Maryland and Virginia in the 1600s. Chincoteagues are feral. They eat dune and marsh grasses. The National Park Service owns the horses on the Maryland side of the island. A fire department owns the horses on the Virginia side. Each year, there is an event where people swim some of the horses across the channel to the mainland. People can buy these horses. This keeps the island horse numbers from growing too large.

Canada

United States

Pacific Ocean

Atlantic Ocean

Mexico

From: The United States of America

The Clydesdale has a broad forehead.

Appearance

The Clydesdale is a heavy draft horse. It has a flat, wide muzzle. It has large nostrils and big ears. Its neck is arched, and its back is short. The horse is stocky and muscular.

Atlantic Ocean

Scotland

Northern Ireland

Ireland

England

Wales

From: Scotland

Most Clydesdales are bay. A Clydesdale can also be black or chestnut. It is usually white from the knees to the hooves. This horse often has a wide, white stripe, or blaze, on its face.

Height: 16.2 to 18 hands

Behavior and Uses

Clydesdales come from Scotland. They were bred to work on farms. These horses also pulled loads for coal miners. Clydesdales are very active. They lift their feet high off the ground with each step. Today, they are used to pull carriages or to ride for fun.

CONNEMARA PONY

Gray is one of the most common colors for Connemaras.

Appearance

The Connemara pony is a large pony breed. The first Connemara was dun. Now the breed can be gray, black, bay, or brown. It has short legs and rounded shoulders.

North Sea

Ireland

United Kingdom

Atlantic Ocean

From: Ireland

This pony has a thick mane and tail. Connemaras can live into their 30s.

Behavior and Uses

Height: 13 to 15 hands

The Connemara comes from Ireland. This pony was used by farmers. It pulled plows and carts. It was a hard worker. Today, the Connemara is known for staying healthy in harsh weather. It can survive on whatever grasses are in the pasture. It is very good at jumping and competes in shows. People also ride Connemaras for fun. This pony is gentle.

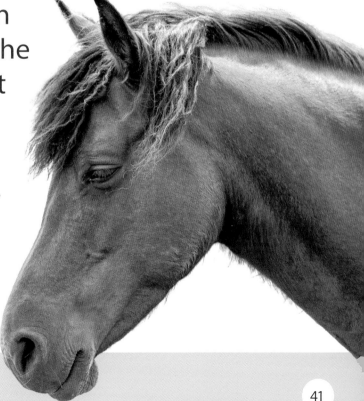

The Criollo has a fast gait.

Appearance

The Criollo is a light riding horse that can be dun, palomino, or chestnut. The horse has a sturdy build. Its mane and tail are thick, and its tail is low set.

Height: 13.3 to 15.3 hands

Behavior and Uses

The Criollo was bred in Argentina from Spanish horses. It works on cattle ranches and farms. People also ride Criollos in rodeos or for fun. The horse is good-natured. It can work hard for a long time. There is a yearly event in Argentina. Criollo owners ride their horses for 14 days. They go 465 miles (750 km). Each horse carries a 250-pound (113 kg) load, including the rider. It eats only what it finds along the trail.

From: Argentina

DUTCH WARMBLOOD

Many Dutch warmbloods are bred to compete at the highest levels.

Appearance

The Dutch warmblood is chestnut, bay, black, or gray. It often has white on its face and legs. The head is straight, and the neck is arched. The back is straight

The Netherlands

North Sea

Germany

Belgium

From: The Netherlands

44

and long. The horse's tail is set high. Its hindquarters are strong and muscular.

Behavior and Uses

Horses can be hot, warm, or cold blooded. These terms describe a horse's nature. A warmblood is smart, calm, and easy to train. The Dutch warmblood is a sport horse. People ride this horse in shows and events such as jumping. The Dutch warmblood is also used for pulling carriages, riding for fun, and helping with farm work.

Height: 16.2 to 17 hands

Children and small adults can ride Exmoor ponies.

Appearance

The Exmoor pony comes in shades of brown. Its legs are darker. It has oatmeal-colored markings on its muzzle, around its eyes, and on its belly. The mane and tail are dark brown. Exmoor ponies are strong and stocky.

Height: 11.2 to 13.1 hands

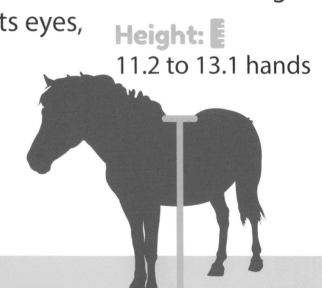

Behavior and Uses

Exmoor is a hilly area in the southwest of England. This pony is thought to have come there between 200,000 and 100,000 years ago. It lives on the grasses in this area. The pony grows a summer coat to keep itself cool. It grows a winter coat to keep itself warm and dry. Today, Exmoor ponies are used for riding, pulling carriages, and jumping.

Atlantic Ocean

Scotland

Northern Ireland

Ireland

England

Wales

From: England

This is the only horse breed from Finland.

Appearance

The Finnish horse is a draft horse. It is usually chestnut and often has white markings on its face and legs. The Finnish horse can also be bay, gray, and sometimes brown or black. Its tail and mane are usually golden.

Height: 14.2 to 15.3 hands

Behavior and Uses

This is a good trotting horse. People use it as a jumping horse and for racing. It can keep up its energy for a long time. The Finnish horse is often used in riding schools because it is calm and patient. It is also a good show jumper. The Finnish horse will pull heavy loads. It is also called the Finnish Universal because it is good at so many things.

From: Finland

The Friesian's tail can grow to the ground.

Appearance

The Friesian horse has a very long tail and mane. The mane and tail are not supposed to be trimmed. The Friesian also has feathering on its legs. Its coat is always black. Sometimes this horse has a white star on its forehead. The Friesian holds its head up high. Its body is muscular.

Height: 15 hands

Behavior and Uses

This horse comes from the Netherlands. The Friesian horse is shown in art from the Middle Ages. It was used by knights in battle. It also pulled coaches for royal families in France and Spain. Today, it is used for light farm work. It pulls carts. It also works in circuses and does driving contests where it pulls carriages. It is good-natured.

The Netherlands

North Sea

Germany

Belgium

From: The Netherlands

Black and white is a common color pattern in the breed.

Appearance

The Gypsy vanner horse is a stocky draft horse with a long mane and tail. It has feathering on its legs. The mane, tail, and feathers are straight and silky. The Gypsy vanner can be black or brown. It usually has patches of one of these colors along with white patches.

Height: 13 to 16 hands

Behavior and Uses

This horse was first used by Romani (formerly called Gypsy) travelers in England in the 1900s. It is called *vanner* for the word *caravan*. It pulled the carts in the Romani caravan. It is known for its strength, good nature, and beauty. It has a lively trot, with or without pulling a load. Because it is gentle, it is often used to teach children to ride.

From: England

Hackneys are shown in many different competitions today.

Appearance

Hackneys are muscular. They have wide chests and arched necks. They are usually dark in color.

Behavior and Uses

This horse comes from England. In the 1800s, roadways were made smoother. They had fewer ruts and holes. This meant farmers did not need heavy draft horses to pull their carts. Wealthy farmers bred Hackney horses as light, fast trotting horses. The horses wore harnesses. The Hackneys raised each leg up high as they trotted to pull a carriage. Today, Hackneys are used as show horses. They tend to be jumpy and nervous. This makes them hard to train and handle.

Height: 14.2 to 15.2 hands

From: England

Haflingers are eager to please.

Appearance

The Haflinger is a small golden-chestnut horse. It has a thick, white or cream tail and mane. It sometimes has white on its face and legs. This horse's body is short and stocky. It is strong and sturdy.

Height: 13.2 to 15 hands

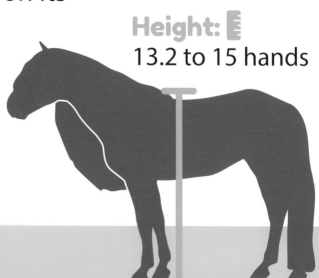

Behavior and Uses

The Haflinger comes from the mountains of Austria in Europe. It carried people and loads up and down narrow mountain paths. This horse is friendly to people. It is very easygoing. It is eager to please. The Haflinger is a good riding horse for children. This horse is also used in shows, jumping, and trail riding. Although it is small, it can carry heavy loads.

From: Austria

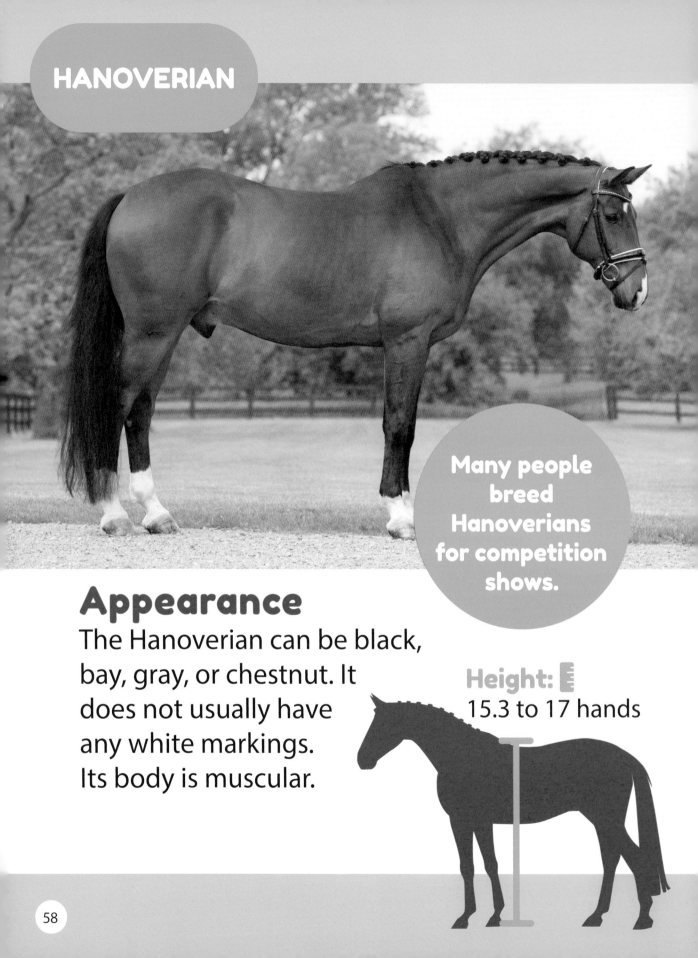

Many people breed Hanoverians for competition shows.

Appearance

The Hanoverian can be black, bay, gray, or chestnut. It does not usually have any white markings. Its body is muscular.

Height: 15.3 to 17 hands

Behavior and Uses

This horse comes from northern Germany. Farmers and soldiers originally used this horse for farm work and riding. It is a warmblood, and it does not get easily excited or upset. It is easy to train. The Hanoverian is good at competing in shows. It is known for its special gaits. It has a light and bouncy walk. When it trots, it looks like it is floating. When it canters, it has a steady rhythm.

From: Germany

HIGHLAND PONY

The Highland pony has powerful back legs.

Appearance

The Highland pony has a stocky body. It has a thick, long mane and tail. This pony can be dun, yellow, gray, or cream. It can also be brown, bay, or chestnut.

Height:
13 to 14.2 hands

The mane and tail are sometimes silver. Often, these horses have stripes on their backs, legs, and shoulders.

Behavior and Uses

Two hundred years ago, the Highland pony was the workhorse for farmers in Scotland. It pulled plows and carried loads. Today, the pony still works on farms. It is also used for riding. It can jump high and be ridden for long distances. It is willing to keep walking when a trail is rough or steep. It is not bothered by stormy weather.

From: Scotland

HOLSTEINER

Holsteiners compete in the top levels of many sports.

Appearance

The Holsteiner is a warmblood and is usually bay with few or no white markings. It can be other solid colors as well. It moves in a light, graceful way.

Behavior and Uses

This horse comes from northern Germany. Farmers first used this horse because it was strong and steady. Soldiers also used it because it was brave and willing to ride into battle. In the 1800s, the Holsteiner was used to pull carriages. In modern times, it is used in shows, for jumping, and for pulling carriages. The Holsteiner is relaxed and willing to work. It is known for its steady feet and powerful hindquarters.

Height: ▤
16 or 17 hands

From: Germany

Icelandic horses are good with children.

Appearance

The Icelandic horse can come in more than 40 colors. The most common color is chestnut. This horse has a thick, long mane and tail. In winter its coat is even thicker.

Behavior and Uses

This horse was used by Vikings in the 800s CE. It carried warriors into battle. The Icelandic horse

also worked on farms and carried carts and heavy loads. Today, this horse is used for riding and sheep roundups. It also appears in shows and contests. It is

Height: 12.3 to 13.1 hands

calm and good-natured. The Icelandic horse has five gaits. It walks, trots, and canters. It also has a running walk. Some have a flying pace. This is a fast gait for short races.

Norwegian Sea

Iceland

Atlantic Ocean

From: Iceland

IRISH DRAUGHT HORSE

In 2022, there were fewer than 1,000 Irish draught horses in the United States.

Appearance

The Irish draught horse can be any solid color. Most are gray or chestnut. This horse has a wide forehead. It has big eyes that are spaced wide. The Irish draught horse has strong legs.

Height: 15.2 to 16.2 hands

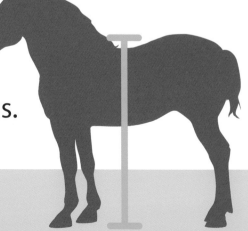

It is lightweight for a draft horse. It has strong hooves. This is important for jumping on hard land.

Behavior and Uses

Irish farmers used this horse starting in the late 1800s and early 1900s. It pulled a plow. This horse also pulled people in a cart. Farmers rode it while hunting. It was known for its lasting power. It was a good jumper. Today, it is a sport horse. It is also used for riding and other events.

Northern Ireland

Ireland

Great Britain

Atlantic Ocean

From: Ireland and Northern Ireland

KNABSTRUPPER

Some Knabstruppers have more spots than others.

Appearance

The Knabstrupper is covered with spots. It can be many different colors. It has large, strong hindquarters. Its head is small. This horse has small, pointed ears. It has a square muzzle and a high-set neck. Its hooves are light or striped.

Height: 15.1 to 16 hands

Behavior and Uses

This horse comes from Denmark. It was used by the Vikings. It was also used by Chinese people to bring silk to France and Spain. Today, it is a riding horse and pulls carriages. It is used in circuses and shows. It competes in events. The Knabstrupper is lively and hardworking. It is easy to train. It is also friendly and gentle.

North Sea

Sweden

Denmark

Germany

Baltic Sea

From: Denmark

LIPIZZAN

Lipizzans are smart.

Appearance

Most Lipizzans are gray. Some are black or bay. They have sturdy bodies. They hold their heads up high. They have big eyes and small, pointed ears. Their necks are short and strong. Their tails and manes are thick and long.

Height: 14.2 to 15.2 hands

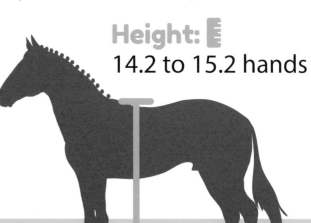

Behavior and Uses

This horse was first bred in Austria in 1580. It comes from Spanish, Arabian, and Berber horses. It was a fast, light horse. It was used in the military. It pulled carriages too. The Spanish Riding School opened in Austria in the 1500s. It is still there today. Its goal is to teach riders the art of riding and training a horse. The school uses only Lipizzan horses.

From: Austria

All Lusitanos born in a certain year are given names that start with the same first letter.

Appearance

The Lusitano is often gray, bay, or chestnut. It has a medium-long head. Its eyes are large and almond shaped. The ears are small, and the tips curve inward. The Lusitano's mane and tail are thick and silky. The neck is thick

Height: Usually 15.1 to 15.3 hands

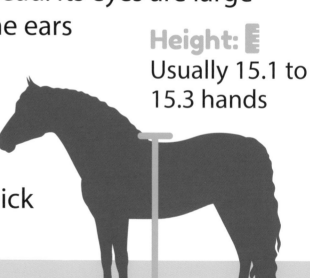

and arched. The back is short and strong. The tail is set low. The body is muscular and powerful.

Behavior and Uses

The Lusitano's ancestors are shown in cave paintings in what is now Spain. The Lusitano horse is kind and gentle. It is smart and willing to work. Today, people in Spain and Portugal still keep these horses. The breed is used for competing, working, and riding.

France

Atlantic Ocean

Spain

Mediterranean Sea

Portugal

Morocco

From: Spain

The Marwari could survive in the desert without much food or water.

Appearance

The Marwari horse has a broad forehead. The ears curve inward at the tips. The Marwari has large, wide-set eyes. It has a broad, deep chest. It has a short back. This horse can be dark brown, bay, chestnut, dun, or gray.

Height: 14 to 15.2 hands

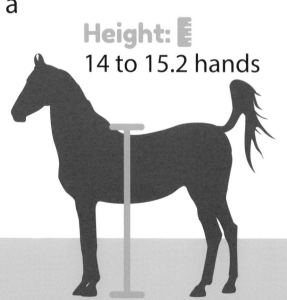

Behavior and Uses

The Marwari comes from India. Warriors used it starting in the 1100s CE. It could survive in the desert without much food or water. Its straighter shoulders let the horse lift its feet above the sand. It was known for bringing back riders who had gotten lost in the desert. The Marwari has a keen sense of hearing. This helps the horse warn its rider of far-off danger. Today, these horses are used for trail riding, shows, and polo games in which riders hit balls with sticks.

From: India

MINIATURE HORSE

People once used miniature horses to work in mines.

Appearance
A miniature horse is very small. But it is built like a horse, with a light body and long legs. So it is not

Atlantic Ocean

Europe

Asia

Africa

From: Europe

considered a pony, which is usually stocky with short legs. A miniature horse can be many different colors.

Behavior and Uses

Height: 8.5 hands or under

Miniature horses can do almost anything larger horses can do. People may keep miniature horses as pets. Miniature horses can also pull carts and be ridden by children. These horses cannot be ridden by people who weigh more than 70 pounds (32 kg). Miniature horses also visit people in hospitals and nursing homes. These horses are smart and curious. They are gentle and easy to train.

MISSOURI FOX TROTTER

The Missouri fox trotter has bright eyes.

Appearance

The Missouri fox trotter has pointed ears. It has a narrow muzzle. The back is short and strong. The chest and rear are muscular. Its hair is soft and silky. It can be many different colors.

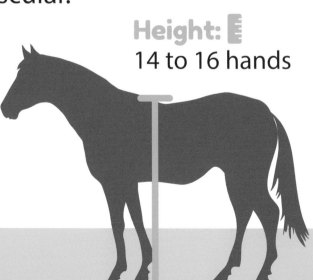

Height: 14 to 16 hands

Behavior and Uses

This horse was used by settlers in the Ozark Mountains of the United States during the 1800s. It could carry riders long distances over rough trails. The Missouri fox trotter has a special gait. It walks in front and trots behind. Its head nods as it moves. Its step is springy but also smooth. It is a comfortable gait to ride. Missouri fox trotters can travel using this gait at a speed of 5 to 8 miles per hour (8 to 13 kmh).

Canada

Pacific
Ocean

United
States

Atlantic
Ocean

Mexico

From: The United States of America

MONGOLIAN

The Mongolian horse plays an important role in the lives of Mongolian people today.

Appearance

The Mongolian has a stocky build. Its legs are thick and short. The horse's head is large, and its neck is short. The Mongolian's mane and tail are thick and long. In winter, the coat grows thick. This horse has strong, hard hooves. It can be any color.

Height: 12 to 14 hands

Behavior and Uses

This horse was used in Mongolia thousands of years ago. It pulled carriages. It carried warriors. The horse could ride long distances across deserts and mountains. Today, the Mongolian is one of the most-used horse breeds in China. People use it for riding and pulling carts. The horse is also used for milk and meat. The Mongolian horse is a strong worker.

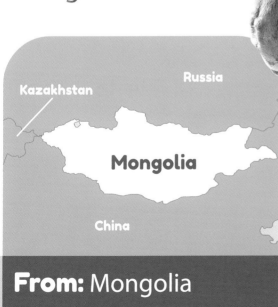

Kazakhstan

Russia

Mongolia

China

From: Mongolia

MORGAN

The Morgan is muscular.

Appearance

The Morgan is a light but powerful horse. It usually comes in chestnut, bay, or brown. But some are black, palomino, buckskin, or gray. This horse holds its head high on a graceful neck. It has big eyes.

Height: 14.2 to 15.2 hands

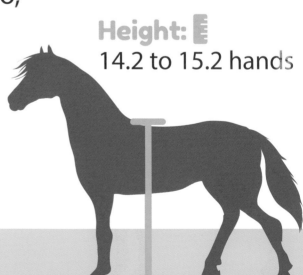

Behavior and Uses

This breed of horse began with Justin Morgan. His horse was named Figure. It was born in Massachusetts in 1789. During its 32-year life, the horse amazed people. Figure worked hard on the farm. He pulled logs and carried people over many miles. He ran fast and was very healthy. Figure was gentle and friendly. Today, Morgans still work on farms. They are used in shows and to pull carriages.

From: The United States of America

Mustangs are good at choosing the safest path over rough ground.

Appearance

Mustangs can be many different sizes, shapes, and colors. They can also have different body types. Most are chestnut and bay. Mustangs are usually light, warmblood horses. They have muscular bodies and hard hooves.

Height: 13 to 16 hands

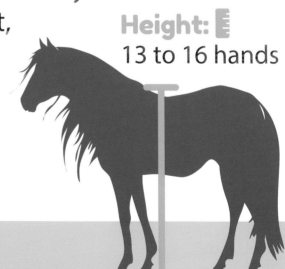

Behavior and Uses

The name *mustang* comes from a Spanish word meaning "wild." Mustangs are the feral horses of the United States. They were first brought to North America by Spanish settlers. They escaped and became wild. They grazed in large herds. Many were later caught and tamed by settlers. Today, mustangs can still be found in herds in the wild. Those that have been caught and tamed are used for riding.

From: The United States of America

NEW FOREST PONY

The New Forest pony is easy to train.

Appearance

The New Forest pony is usually bay, brown, or gray. Sometimes it is chestnut, roan, or black. Some ponies have small, white markings on their heads or legs.

Height: 13.2 to 15 hands

Behavior and Uses

This breed comes from a forest in southern England. There are still wild ponies in the region. People also own New Forest ponies. This breed is smart, strong, quiet, and easygoing. It is very comfortable around people. Children and small adults use it for riding. This pony is a good jumper. It pulls carriages. It is used in shows and long-distance riding. It is a fast racer even over rough trails.

Atlantic Ocean

Scotland

Northern Ireland

Ireland

England

Wales

From: England

NORWEGIAN FJORD HORSE

The Norwegian fjord horse is a good horse for children or beginning riders.

Appearance

The Norwegian fjord horse's coat is dun. It has a dark stripe that starts at the forehead and runs along the back to the tail. It has dark bars on the legs. It has black lower legs.

Height: 13 to 14.1 hands

Behavior and Uses

This is Norway's oldest horse breed. The breed has been there for more than 2,000 years. Vikings used it in battle. People also used it for farming. Today, it is known for being dependable. It is calm and gentle. It is easy to train. The Norwegian fjord horse can be ridden with a saddle. It can pull a cart. It is also used for shows, parades, and jumping.

From: Norway

89

OLDENBURG

The Oldenburg Breeding Society keeps track of this breed.

Appearance

The Oldenburg has a big frame with a high-set neck. Its legs are long. The horse is muscular. It has a long stride. This warmblood's gait is bouncy and lively. Most are black, brown, bay, chestnut, or gray.

Height: 16 to 17.2 hands

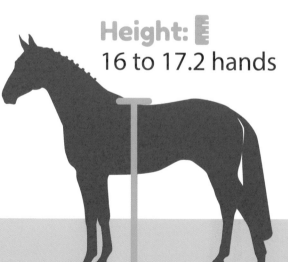

Behavior and Uses

This horse comes from northwestern Germany. Farmers bred it as a high-stepping carriage horse in the 1600s. Wealthy people used it to pull fancy carriages. When cars were invented, horses were not needed as much.

People began to use the horse for sports and fun. It is gentle and willing to work. It is a good jumper. It is also still used to pull carriages.

North Sea
Denmark
Baltic Sea
The Netherlands
Poland
Germany
Belgium
Czechia
Luxembourg
France
Austria
Switzerland

From: Germany

The Orlov trotter is strong.

Appearance

The Orlov trotter can be gray, bay, black, or chestnut. It has a big head, large eyes, and a long, arched neck. The chest is deep and wide. The horse's body is muscular. Its back is long.

Height: 15.7 to 15.9 hands

Behavior and Uses

This horse was bred in the late 1700s in central Russia. This area has harsh weather. The roads are rough. Towns are far apart. The Orlov trotter was able to work in these conditions. It is a fast harness horse. It can keep working for a long time. It is used as a draft horse. The Orlov trotter is a workhorse on farms. People also ride it for fun and in shows.

From: Russia

The Paso Fino carries its neck high.

Appearance

The Paso Fino's head is straight and medium-sized. Its eyes are large and alert. Its ears are short and curve inward at

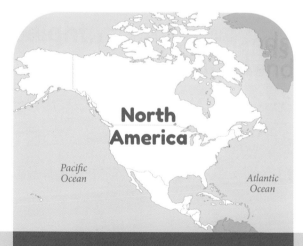

North America

Pacific Ocean

Atlantic Ocean

From: North America

94

the tips. Its neck is arched. This horse's back is muscular. Its legs are straight. The mane and tail are long and thick. The Paso Fino can be any color.

Height:
13 to 15.2 hands

Behavior and Uses

This horse comes from the first horses Christopher Columbus brought to North America in the 1490s. It is friendly and hardworking. It is gentle and calm. This horse is named for its special gait. *Paso Fino* means "fine step" in Spanish. Its gait has a four-beat rhythm. Paso Finos are found throughout North and South America. They are used for shows, trail riding, and ranch work.

PERCHERON

Percherons are powerful.

Appearance

The Percheron is gray or black. It has a springy gait. Its forehead is wide. The horse's eyes are bright, and its nostrils are wide. It is muscular. The Percheron has a long neck and a thick mane. The tail is set high. The back is short and straight.

Height: 14.3 to 16.2 hands

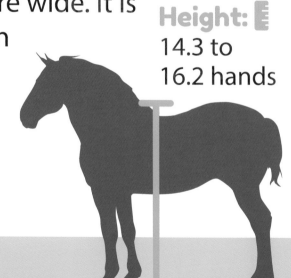

Behavior and Uses

This horse comes from French and Arab horses that lived before the Middle Ages. The breed started in France. Farmers used it for plowing. The horse also pulled carts for merchants. Today, Percherons are used on small farms. They pull logs for forest workers. People also use them for hayrides or sleighrides and in parades. At fairs, Percherons compete in hitching and halter contests.

From: France

This breed is gentle and calm.

Appearance

The Pony of the Americas is a large pony. It is built more like a horse. This pony's coat can have different patterns and spots. Its eyes have white around the colored center. Its skin is spotted. The pony's hooves are striped.

Height:
11 to 14 hands

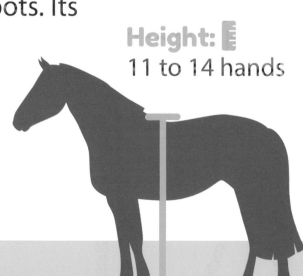

Behavior and Uses

This pony was first bred in 1954 in Iowa. It was meant to be a pretty, fast, hardworking horse. It was bred for riders who were too big for a small pony but not yet ready for a horse. It is smart and patient. It is easy to train. This pony works well in shows and jumping events.

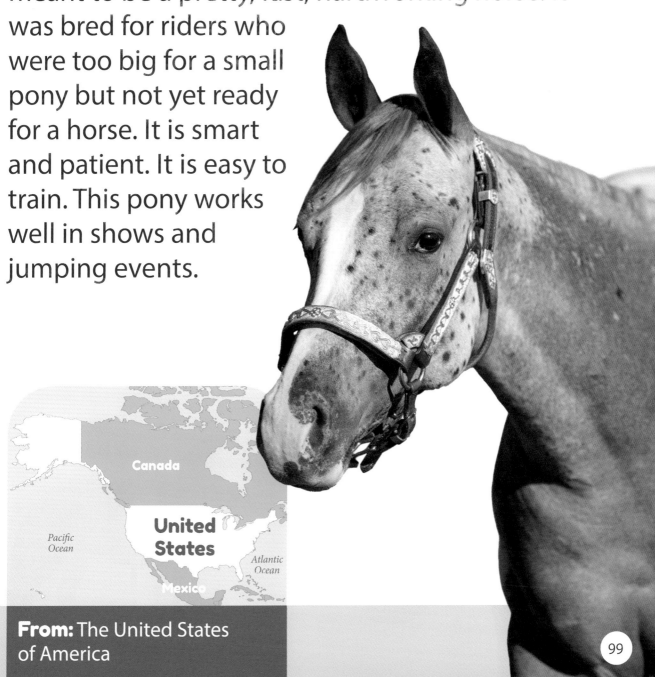

Canada

United States

Pacific Ocean

Atlantic Ocean

Mexico

From: The United States of America

99

This horse is called *takhi*, meaning "spirit" or "holy" in Mongolian.

Appearance

The Przewalski's (shuh-VAHL-skeez) horse usually comes in tan, dun, and reddish bay. It has a stripe down its back. It also has a shoulder stripe and stripes on its legs. Its muzzle and belly are lighter than the rest of its coat. Its mane and tail are dark. The mane stands up.

Height: 12 to 14 hands

Behavior and Uses

This is the last living wild horse. It has never been tamed. Pictures of Przewalski's horses can be found in cave paintings 30,000 years old. When people began farming, the horses were a problem. They broke fences and ate crops. Many were killed. Today, the largest herd is in southern Russia. Zoos breed these horses to help increase the wild population.

From: Europe and Asia

ROCKY MOUNTAIN HORSE

These horses are easy to train.

Appearance

The Rocky Mountain horse has a wide chest. It has a solid-colored coat. The horse sometimes has a few white markings on its face.

Behavior and Uses

This breed began in Kentucky in the late 1800s.

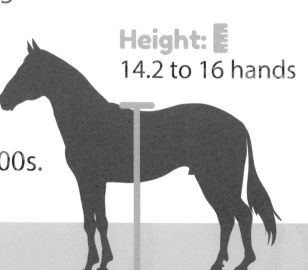

Height: 14.2 to 16 hands

It was known for its gentle nature. Farmers used it for many things. It pulled plows and moved cattle. Children and adults both rode it. The horse could also pull a buggy. It was comfortable in cold winter weather. Today, Rocky Mountain horses are used for riding. They are good for trail riding and shows. This horse moves with a relaxed, four-beat gait. It still drives cattle. Rocky Mountain horses can go long distances without getting tired.

From: The United States of America

SHAGYA ARABIAN

The breed gets its name from a male horse of the breed born in 1810, Shagya.

Appearance

The Shagya Arabian has a broad, muscular chest. It is often gray. It can also be chestnut, bay, or white. This horse is taller than the Arabian.

Height: 15 to 16 hands

Behavior and Uses

The Shagya Arabian comes from Hungary. It was bred in 1789 using Arabians, Thoroughbreds, and Lipizzans. It was used as a warhorse and to pull a carriage. The breed is rare. Today, it is used as a sport horse. It is good at jumping, showing, and pulling carriages. It is also ridden for fun. This horse is known for being tough and friendly.

From: Hungary

SHETLAND PONY

The Shetland's small size made it good for pulling carts in coal mines.

Appearance

The Shetland pony has a shaggy coat. Its mane, tail, and forelock are thick and long. Its body is short and muscular. Most Shetland ponies are black or dark brown. A Shetland pony's coat color can change with the seasons.

Height: 9.3 to 10.2 hands

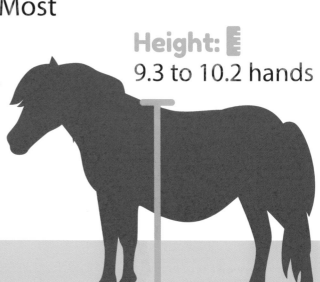

Behavior and Uses

This pony comes from the Shetland Islands of Scotland. It is cold there. The pony carried peat, a material found in wet soil. People burned it for fuel. These ponies also carried seaweed from the shore to people's farms. The seaweed was added to the soil to help plants grow. Today, Shetlands are kept as pets. Children can ride them. The ponies also pull small carts.

From: Shetland Islands

This breed is named for the rural English counties called shires.

Appearance

The shire can weigh 2,000 pounds (900 kg). It has long, thick feathering that extends down from the knee and spreads around the hoof. The shire's coat is usually bay, brown, black, gray, or chestnut.

Height: 17 hands

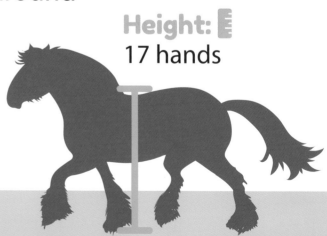

Behavior and Uses

This horse comes from England. It is also called the "English great horse." Hundreds of years ago, it carried knights into battle. The shire horse's large, muscular body was able to hold the weight of a man and his armor. These horses also worked on farms and pulled carts with heavy loads. They were known for their strength and good nature. Today, the shire horse is used as a workhorse and for riding.

Atlantic Ocean

Scotland

Northern Ireland

Ireland

England

Wales

From: England

SORRAIA

All Sorraias came from just 11 or 12 horses that were captured in the 1930s.

Appearance

The Sorraia is a small horse. Its legs are too long for it to be a pony. This horse is dun or grullo, a mousy color. It has a dark face and muzzle. It has a black stripe down the back and black ear tips. The legs have stripes. Sometimes the shoulders

Height: ▤
14 hands

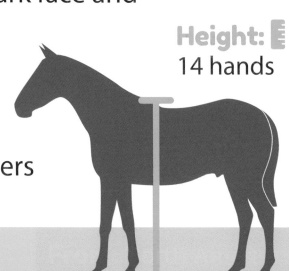

have stripes too. The mane and tail are black with some lighter hairs.

Behavior and Uses

The Sorraia horse lived in the wild in Portugal before the early 1900s. Its origins are uncertain. Today, there are only about 200 Sorraias. This breed is at risk of dying out. People protect them in special areas. Some of these horses have been tamed to ride. People use some to move livestock.

Portugal

Spain

Atlantic Ocean

Morocco

From: Portugal

Spanish barbs have strong legs.

Appearance

The Spanish barb is a light riding horse. It has a broad forehead and small muzzle. The neck is arched. The back is short to medium. This horse's legs are medium long. It has tough hooves. The mane and tail

From: Spain

are thick. Barbs can be black, sorrel, chestnut, roan, dun, or buckskin.

Behavior and Uses

More than 1,000 years ago, soldiers from Africa rode barbs when they invaded Spain. These horses and Spanish horses mixed together. The Spanish barb was created. Later, Europeans brought Spanish barbs to North America. The horses were used in wars. They helped with work on ranches. Barbs are energetic and spirited. They make good family horses.

Height:
14 to 15 hands

This breed is said to be the fastest harness horse in the world.

Appearance

The Standardbred has a long body and a medium-sized neck. It is muscular and lean. It can be bay, brown, or black.

Behavior and Uses

This breed comes from an English Thoroughbred

Height: 15.2 hands

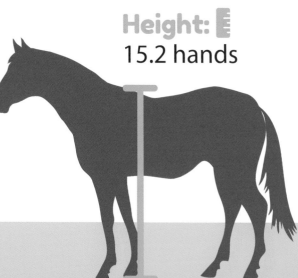

named Messenger born in 1780. He was brought to the United States. The Standardbred has a special gait called the pace. When it paces, it puts its weight on the left front and back legs. It moves the right front and back legs together. Then it moves both left legs.

The Standardbred is a harness horse. A harness horse pulls a two-wheeled cart in races. The first harness races were done on country roads. Today, there are special racetracks. Standardbreds are often gentle and patient.

From: The United States of America

Suffolk punches are calm.

Appearance

The Suffolk punch is a draft horse. It comes in shades of chestnut, from light gold to dark brown. It might have a white star or white ankles. It weighs up to 1,800 pounds (817 kg). Its body is

Height: Usually 16.1 hands

muscular and rounded. This horse's legs are short. It has big, round hooves.

Behavior and Uses

Farmers in eastern England used this horse to do heavy work in the 1500s. It pulled a plow through heavy soil. Suffolk punches were less in demand after the growing use of farm machinery with engines in the mid-1900s. They are rare today. This horse is strong and dependable. It is easy to work with.

Atlantic Ocean

Scotland

Northern Ireland

Ireland

England

Wales

From: England

TENNESSEE WALKING HORSE

This breed is sure-footed, smart, and strong.

Appearance

The Tennessee walking horse comes in many colors. It can be brown, black, bay, chestnut, roan, palomino, white, or gray. It sometimes has white markings on its face, legs, and body. This horse has a long neck.

Height: 14.3 to 17 hands

It has a short back, bright eyes, and pointed ears. Its tail and mane are long.

Behavior and Uses

Sometimes, this horse has a special gait. It looks like a smooth, fast running walk. The head bobs with each step. Tennessee walkers can do this at 10 to 20 miles per hour (16 to 32 kmh). Some horses swing their ears or snap their teeth with each step. Only some horses of the breed are born able to do this running walk.

From: The United States of America

THOROUGHBRED

Many racing Thoroughbreds later compete in other sports.

Appearance

The Thoroughbred has wide-set eyes. Its neck is long and slender. The Thoroughbred has high withers and a curved back. This horse is muscular. Coat colors are bay, dark bay, chestnut, black, or gray. Often, this horse has white markings on its face and legs.

Height: 16 hands

Behavior and Uses

All Thoroughbreds are related to one of three male horses. These three horses were from the Middle East. They came to England in the early 1600s. They were good at running fast over long distances while carrying riders. Thoroughbreds are used in races. They are also used for jumping, shows, and polo. The breed is spirited.

Atlantic Ocean

Scotland

Northern Ireland

Ireland

England

Wales

From: England

Trakehners look like they float when they move.

Appearance

The Trakehner has a light, bouncy trot. It has a lean, muscular body. It can be any solid color. It is known for its good nature and beauty. This horse is said to look elegant and noble.

Behavior and Uses

This warmblood was first bred in what are now

Height: 16 to 17 hands

Germany and Russia in 1732. In 1945, war forced some people to flee west. Trakehners pulled their wagons. Today, Trakehners are used for shows and jumping. Trakehners have won medals for the US Dressage Team in the Olympics. They are also used for work and riding.

Germany

Russia

Poland

Ukraine

China

Kazakhstan

Mongolia

From: Germany, Russia, and surrounding area

WELSH PONY AND COB

The Welsh pony and cob has a fast trot.

Appearance

The Welsh pony and cob comes in four types. The two Welsh pony types are light but sturdy. The Welsh cob is larger and stockier. The Welsh pony of cob type is stockier than the pony

Height:
Welsh pony:
under 14.2 hands
Welsh pony of cob:
up to 13.2 hands
Welsh cob:
over 13.2 hands

types but lighter than the cob. This breed has large eyes and small ears. Its tail is set high.

Behavior and Uses

This pony comes from Wales. The area is cold. Thousands of years ago, this pony ran wild. It was tough. When tamed, it pulled carriages. It worked in coal mines. It was used for ranch work. Today, it is used as a family horse. It can live outdoors all year. It is a good jumper.

From: Wales

GLOSSARY

ancestor
A family member from an earlier time.

bred
Brought two animals together to have young.

breed
A group of animals that looks and acts similarly.

dressage
The sport of riding a horse while it responds to very small cues.

feathering
Long hair on the lower legs.

feral
An escaped domestic animal that has become wild, and its offspring.

gait
A pattern of moving the feet; in horses, the walk, trot, and canter are different gaits.

herd
A group of animals that stays together.

hoof
The hard covering on a horse's foot.

mane
Hair growing from the neck of a horse.

muzzle
The mouth, nose, chin, and lips.

pasture
A grassy field for animals.

saddle
A padded leather seat for a rider.

stocky
Thick in build.

warmblood
An athletic horse that is usually calm and easily trained.

withers
The ridge between a horse's shoulder bones.

TO LEARN MORE

More Books to Read

Halls, Kelly Milner. *All about Horses: A Kid's Guide to Breeds, Care, Riding, and More!* Rockridge, 2021.

Laboucarie, Sandra. *The Ultimate Book of Horses.* Twirl, 2020.

Mills, Andrea. *The Everything Book of Horses and Ponies.* DK, 2019.

Online Resources

Booklinks
NONFICTION NETWORK
FREE ONLINE NONFICTION RESOURCES

To learn more about horses, please visit **abdobooklinks.com** or scan this QR code. These links are routinely monitored and updated to provide the most current information available.

INDEX

PHOTO CREDITS